Carolina Gold Rice

Carolina Gold Rice

The Ebb and Flow History of a Lowcountry Cash Crop

Richard Schulze

Foreword by John Martin Taylor

Charleston   London

the
History
PRESS

Published by The History Press
18 Percy Street
Charleston, SC 29403
866.223.5778
www.historypress.net

Cover: A watercolor by the author's wife, Tricia Schulze.

First published 2005
Manufactured in the United Kingdom
1.59629.094.3

Library of Congress Cataloging-in-Publication Data
Schulze, Richard, 1934-
Carolina gold rice : the ebb and flow history of a lowcountry
cash crop /
Richard Schulze ; with a foreword by John Martin Taylor.
p. cm.
Includes bibliographical references.
ISBN 1-59629-094-3
1.   Rice--South Carolina--History. 2. Cash crops--South
Carolina--History.
I. Title.
SB191.R5S372 2005
633.1'8'09757--dc22
                              2005023976

Contents

Foreword

*H*is roots are Texan and he lives large with plantations, hunting trips and safaris, vintage roadsters and the speedboat. But Dick Schulze has also practiced with precision and skill the delicate operations of eye surgery for thirty years. He has made such an impact on my own stomping grounds, the fabled Lowcountry of South Carolina and Georgia, that I can't think of him as anything other than a Sandlapper—one of us. He's also a farmer who has learned that all the precision and skill in the world won't keep the ricebirds out of the fields or the rains away during harvest.

It has been nearly twenty years now since first we met. I was researching the rich culinary history of the Lowcountry and everyone told me that I should meet Dick and Tricia Schulze, who were planting the once great, but then nearly forgotten, Carolina Gold rice. The heir apparent to Middleburg Plantation, South Carolina's oldest home, Macky Hill provided my introduction, and I drove from Charleston on the sinuous and live-oak-canopied two-lane blacktops down to the Schulze plantation, Turnbridge, just outside Savannah on the Carolina side of the river. It was late summer and they were getting ready to harvest their legendary crop of 1988.

Dick's bright eyes reflected his passion. His arms proudly spread out over his golden, ripe fields of grain. He talked about the land with a historian's perspective, a doctor's grasp of biology, a hunter's love of the outdoors and a farmer's practicality. He praised the early Native Americans of Turnbridge, the Guale, whose pottery shards we stumbled upon. He cursed the Army Corps of Engineers, whose manipulations of local waters had turned them brackish. We shared delight at the sight of a stray roseate spoonbill on one of the alligator ponds on the property, several hundred miles north of its normal range. We were aghast at the mass of bobolinks (ricebirds) in the fields, which until recently were not common in the area. It began raining, but Tricia drove with abandon through the muck, their golden retrievers at her side. Their only fear of water moccasins seemed to be for their dogs, which they doted on. I immediately liked the Schulzes. How could I not? I had grown up with scientist parents, and not since childhood had I met others with such ebullient curiosity about the world around them.

The fall harvest was awesome. I joined Dick and Tricia in planning their celebratory feast, and each dish would feature rice, the first real Carolina Gold rice harvested in South Carolina in sixty years—something truly worth celebrating, and a moment in history worth writing about. I called my editor at the New York Times and she agreed. On December 28, they ran my story on the front page of the Living section, complete with a photo of Tricia in the rice *fields with one of their dogs. Another photo featured Julius Bing, a neighbor to whom the Schulzes would always give ample credit for his help in the endeavor.*

I've spent many evenings since with the Schulzes, and marveled at their unbridled passion for life. Carolina Gold is just one of many of their muses. I watched them build Hoover, their quail plantation twenty miles north of Turnbridge, where traditional crops such as benne (sesame) are planted in succession for the birds' peculiar diets. I saw Dick have his mason build a wall with numerous different mortar mixes, each slightly different in color, so that he and Tricia could observe the color as it aged, before they chose the right one to use in the building of their new home. I've watched them nurture an oak alley as though it were even more precious than their heirloom rice. I've shared bottles of wine with them in the birding tower of the guesthouse at Turnbridge, everyone stunned by an exceptional sunset. And I've water-skied with them on the Fourth of July, an old Lowcountry test of those of us supposedly over the hill.

The book you hold in your hand is Dick's story. Typically, he tells it without drawing much attention to himself. It's the tale of a gentleman farmer, a sportsman who claims to be in the midst of "retiring." I'm reminded of George Washington in his latter years at Mount Vernon, when he dove into various experiments in farming, manufacturing and commerce. Both traditionalists, Schulze and Washington knew that perhaps the best way to preserve a culture is to do something new with it. To begin again.

I've been telling Dick Schulze's story for years. Now it's his turn.

John Martin Taylor

of Hoppin' John's Lowcountry Cooking

Acknowledgements

To all of my friends mentioned in this book, I give them thanks. Without them, our project would never have succeeded.

Steve Hoffius, Beverly McGhee and Yvette Barnes were most helpful in guiding me through the manuscript.

But most of all, my thanks to Tricia.

A Note on Illustrations

*T*he illustrations in this book are by renowned wildlife artist Floyd Robbins. He lives on Turnbridge Plantation in South Carolina, surrounded by his subjects, and absorbs the beauty around him that shows in his artwork. His principal art form is woodcarving from a solid piece of wood that is transformed into a gorgeous life-like bird in its natural habitat. On sight, one is compelled to touch it to make sure that it doesn't fly away.

Robbins also does watercolors, bronzes and drawings.

Carolina Gold Rice

Part I

The Rise and Fall of Carolina Gold

*T*he story of Carolina Gold rice, from its introduction into the colony of South Carolina until the final demise of the industry and culture, is shrouded in mysteries and misconceptions. Certainly its origins are unclear. Rice, oryza savita, has been the principal cereal of mankind for uncounted years. The remains of cultivated rice dating from around 5000 BC have been identified in eastern China and northern India. Over the following seven millennia, rice spread throughout the world.

When and from where rice was initially brought into South Carolina is not at all clear. Sir William Berkeley, the governor of Virginia, first introduced rice to the colonies in 1647. Since there was an active trade between the colonies, it is reasonable to assume that some rice may have entered the Lowcountry of coastal South Carolina through that route. However, since rice cultivation in Virginia was not a success and there is no documentation of rice growing in the Carolinas before the end of the 1600s, any attempts would have been abortive. There is, however, ample documentation that the Lords Proprietors, the titled financial backers of the colony, desired the introduction of rice from the inception of the colony and early attempts at cultivation were made. Since rice is somewhat difficult to grow, harvest and process, a rice industry would not have suddenly flourished.

Traditionally, it has been thought that the first successful introduction of rice into the Carolina colony occurred in 1685, when a Liverpool-bound brigantine sailing from Madagascar was badly damaged by a storm and blown off course; it set into the port of Charles Towne for repairs. The ship, which was of American origin, was probably not legally trading, as the British law at that time forbade trade outside of the colonies and the British Isles. The vessel, a two-masted and square-rigged vessel, most likely encountered a tropical storm during the summer months. Dr. Henry Woodward apparently befriended the captain, John Thurber, because the records show that he gave a "gentleman of the name of Woodward" a peck of seed rice. According to A.S. Salley Jr., a historian who researched the subject, Woodward proceeded to grow this in his garden in the city and was able in a short time to produce a very good crop, which he then distributed to friends to plant.

Dr. Henry Woodward, a ship's surgeon, was a man of remarkable achievements. Arriving in Barbados at the age of nineteen in 1665, he joined the Barbadians near the Cape Fear River in North Carolina. With Robert Sanford, he then sailed to Port Royal to explore the coast of South Carolina in 1666. After Sanford's departure, he remained behind to live with the Indians for about a year until he was captured by Spaniards and taken to St. Augustine. There he was rescued, only to be subsequently shipwrecked. Finally he arrived back in Charles

Towne Harbor in 1670 as a proprietor's deputy. Understanding the importance of trade with the Indians, as well as wanting them to serve as an effective buffer between South Carolina and the Spaniards at St. Augustine, Lord Ashley Cooper, one of the Lords Proprietors, ordered Dr. Woodward to explore the interior and negotiate alliances and trade agreements. These efforts were viewed as of such importance that Dr. Woodward was even supplied with a secret code to report on his efforts.

For his successful service to the colony, Woodward was granted by the Lords Proprietors the title to two thousand acres of his choosing. He selected a tract on the Abbapoola Creek just off the Stono River on Johns Island. No trace remains of the Abbapoola Plantation.

The details of Dr. Woodward's role in the introduction of rice is not at all clear. Assuming that Thurber's ship entered the port during the summer months, a year would have passed before a new growing season would have allowed the seed to be cultivated. Although tradition holds that Woodward grew the rice in his garden in Charles Towne, it is more likely that it was, in fact, grown at his more suitable property on the Abbapoola Creek. During 1685, the year he was presented the rice, Woodward spent much of his time in the Carolina trading frontier. There he came down with the fever at an Indian village and was evacuated to his plantation where he died at age forty. Thus, it is likely that he was involved with rice cultivation for only one or two seasons. He probably never had the opportunity to fully appreciate the *new industry that he was so instrumental in spawning. Remarkably, no monument has ever been erected to Dr. Henry Woodward, nor has any significant site been named for him.*

Giving credence to the theory that Captain Thurber may indeed have brought the first successful rice seed to Carolina is the fact that in 1715, according to Salley, a poorer Captain Thurber returned to South Carolina seeking a gratuity for "the great benefit that the province had derived from the rice seed which he had brought thereto." The Commons House of Assembly of South Carolina recognized his contribution and granted Thurber a gratuity of one hundred pounds for bringing the first Madagascar rice into the colony. Two years later, Captain John Thurber, age sixty-eight, died and was interred in Warren, Rhode Island.

The second documented introduction of seed rice took place in the year 1696, when Charles Dubois, the treasurer of the East India Company, sent a moneybag to Carolina full of rice. Shortly thereafter, other varieties were introduced from throughout Asia, Europe and Africa, and it seems almost certain that slaves brought their own local varieties with them. Indeed, throughout the whole era of the Carolina rice industry, experiments were conducted with a wide array of varieties. For instance, President Thomas Jefferson presented the South Carolina Agricultural Society with ninety-eight different kinds of rice seed. In spite of the diverse varieties of rice introduced,

it appears that the original seed, which had a golden hue when ripe, became known as "Carolina Gold," though this is not at all certain. In fact, the term "Carolina Gold" was not in use until the period immediately preceding the American Revolution. Whatever its origin, whether the Madagascar seed or a variety derived from one of the multiple introductions that followed, Carolina Gold became the most celebrated variety. The very mystique of its origin adds to its allure.

Recently, research scientists have been able to crack the genetic code for rice. Armed with this knowledge, they soon may be able to trace the origin of Carolina Gold and either confirm or disprove its provenance as Madagascar seed.

Once established, rice became for a time the second most important source of revenue for the colonies behind tobacco. For the Lowcountry, it provided the basis for rapid economic expansion. Unfortunately, it also resulted in the commitment to one-crop agriculture, as well as to slavery—factors that later led to the industry's demise. The colony had been established to make a profit, and profit-producing enterprises had to be found and developed. Rice certainly succeeded in that respect. Remarkably, historical statistics indicate that in 1698, 10,407 pounds of rice were exported; in 1699, 131,207 pounds; and in 1700, 394,130 pounds. This was an almost forty-fold increase in only three years. It is alleged that in 1700, the volume of rice waiting on Charleston docks for export overwhelmed the available ships.

Just as tobacco had given Maryland and Virginia the impetus for an explosive growth in population (both white and black), as well as their economies, so rice quickly became by far the most important segment of the local economy and provided South Carolina with the same vigorous economic growth. In 1747, for instance, rice accounted for 55 percent of the total export value from Carolina, with deerskins and indigo accounting for 22 and 10 percent, respectively. Very soon the industry matured, though it was always vulnerable to extreme cyclical swings due to such factors as crop failures or overproduction, favorable and unfavorable weather, as well as changing international policies and economies. Year-to-year price fluctuations of 100 to 200 percent were not uncommon.

Rice is not an easy crop to produce. While it can be grown on dry ground, it only really flourishes when it can be periodically inundated with salt-free water. This requires a reliable source of water, as well as a means of placing water on the rice and then removing it until the cultivated field becomes dry enough to work. This in turn requires the construction of impoundments, as well as water-control structures that allow for the ingress and egress of water.

Initially, rice fields were constructed on the so-called "reserve system" on the edge of inland swamps. This was a remarkably labor-intensive enterprise, as were all aspects of the colonial rice industry, requiring the damming of an upstream source of water, followed by the laying out of a downstream field, which was then drained, impounded and cleared. Water valves known as "trunks" were placed between the water source and the field, as well as in the outflow drainage ditch. This was the only means of rice production until the mid-1750s. By their very nature, these fields were limited to the upper region of the estuaries and were ordinarily quite small.

A more ambitious scheme of rice growing, known as the "tidal-flow system," was first described in 1748. A tidal-flow rice plantation can be thought of as a massive hydraulic machine consisting of an elaborate system of dikes, canals, drainage ditches and water-control structures. Rather than relying on a higher source of water, the tidal-flow system took advantage of the daily rise and fall of the river water outside the banks so that large amounts of water could be rapidly exchanged in the fields. This system allowed for more frequent flooding and drainage of the fields and was much more reliable.

Along about three hundred miles of the southeast coast, sixteen rivers from Cape Fear to St. Mary's have at least four feet of tide. In all of these coastal estuaries, this zone, where the rise and fall of fresh water is significantly affected by tidal action, is approximately twenty miles wide. Salt is deadly to rice, so rice cultivation is impossible where brackish water exists. However, because fresh water tends to float over the so-called salt wedge, some rice fields could be placed remarkably close to the sea. Likewise, the upper limit of the zone is determined by the degree of tidal effect, with a minimum tidal amplitude of about three feet being required. Compounding the problem with tidal-flow culture were seasonal floods or freshets, which challenged the impoundments from upstream, as well as storm-driven high tides from the sea.

The physical labor necessary for construction and maintenance of this system was enormous, even more so than in the reserve system. The appropriate areas usually originated in cypress swamps where massive trees had to be felled and removed. When possible, stumps were grubbed out by hand and removed by oxen or mules shod with boots to help them stand in the muck. In the same manner, the ditches and banks around the fields were hand-dug. As the banks were, for the most part, built of *highly organic dirt from the site, they were the weak link in what was often a sophisticated engineering feat. The soft material of old dikes was quite vulnerable to storm and flood damage. In fact, due to the peaty nature of the soil, they were even vulnerable to fire. The water-control structures commonly referred to as "trunks" were originally just that, hollow logs used as pipes, which could be blocked or opened as required. Within a few years, more sophisticated water-control structures were built of pegged heart cypress, which is quite impervious to water degradation. These structures were ingenious in design and were critical to the management of the crop, as the delivery and drainage of the water required precise control. Trunks, which functioned as flood gates, evolved to become plank tunnels*

twenty to thirty feet long with swinging gates at each end, set about eleven degrees off vertical. These could be set to either impede or enable water flow. To flood a field, the outside gate was raised and the higher water level pushed open the inside gate so that the water rushed in. When the outside level began to fall, the inner gate flaps closed, trapping the water. To drain a field, or lower the water level, the reverse procedure was followed.

The first phase of rice production occurred in winter after a hard-killing frost. The stubble was cleanly burned to remove excess vegetable matter, which might promote insect growth. Ordinarily, no fertilizer other than the ash from the burned straw was employed. In the spring, dry fields were prepared for planting using beasts of burden, lightly plowing the soft soil. Handwork with hoes completed the preparation of a seedbed. Planting began as early as March or as late as June, the time being dictated by the weather or the experience of the planter. A major consideration for the time of planting was the desire to escape the predation of ricebirds, known locally as May birds, or more properly as bobolinks. These colorful members of the blackbird family would arrive in swarms in May, and if the rice seed had not already germinated, they could seriously compromise the crop yield.

Only the best clean rice seed was used for planting. Originally, seed was sown on the surface of the soil and then in later years a

planting device known as a drill was employed and set to deliver two and a half bushels to the acre. Alternatively, seed that had been "clayed" was broadcast over a shallow layer of water. Since dry rice seed floats, clayed rice was first weighted down by immersion in a slurry of clay mud and then dried.

Irrigation of the field began immediately with inundation of the dry seedbed or, conversely, reversed with the planting of the clayed seed. Then came the appropriately known "sprout flow." The sprout water, which aided the germination of the crop, also had the advantage of destroying some of the competing weeds. It was kept on the field for a few days and then drained. Following this, the sprouted or "pipped" rice was allowed to grow exposed to the sun, while hand hoeing and cultivation took place.

Once the blades of rice were well established and two leaves developed, a second flooding known as the "stretch flow," or "long flow," was initiated. In this case, the water was gradually let into the field to follow the tip of the growing plant. The water level was then elevated to completely cover the plant, thereby floating weeds, debris and insects away from the plant. This detritus was then raked from the edges of the field and left to dry on the banks to be subsequently burned. Water was then gradually removed, and additional hoeing of the crop and cleaning of the drainage ditches took place.

After several weeks of growth on the dry field, a final inundation known as the "harvest flow," or "lay by flow," was put on. The purpose of this flooding was to help the plant stems support the heavy heads of grain as they ripened. Gradually, then, after a couple of months, the final drainage of the now mature crop took place. At last, weather permitting, the crop was ready to be harvested, ordinarily in September.

As with other aspects of rice growing, the harvest itself was highly labor intensive. The plants were cut by hand with sickles, known as "rice hooks." Once cut, they were tied in sheaves, which were then stacked and left to dry in the field, and then transported to high land on wagons or flat-bottom barges where the threshing took place. This involved separating the rice heads, known as "paddy," from the stalks. Originally, this was laboriously done with flailing sticks. Not until the early 1830s were mechanical threshing mills perfected, but they were not widely used for another fifty years.

The rice paddy then required cleaning, a process either performed with screens or by winnowing. This was originally done in an elevated barn with a grated floor. Paddy was poured through the grating where it dropped to a clean surface below. The passing wind removed the chafe. In earlier times, fanner baskets, often made of reeds, were used to perform the same function. Ultimately this too was done by mechanical mills.

Once the cleaned rice or paddy was collected, it was then ready to be pounded or milled. This was done by pounding a small quantity with a wooden mortar and pestle. This process often took a worker, usually a slave, one hour to clean one bushel. Later, water-powered mechanical mills were developed, but were then superseded by steam-engine pounding mills, the first built in 1801 by Jonathan Lucas.

Lucas, who contributed as much to the rice industry as Eli Whitney did to cotton, arrived in America shipwrecked near the mouth of the Santee River in about 1784. An educated millwright, Lucas observed the laborious task of manually threshing and pounding rice and became interested in developing a mechanical means of accomplishing this. In 1787, James Bowman of Peachtree Plantation was the first to engage Lucas to design and construct a water-powered rice mill. Lucas shortly thereafter built rice mills along the Winyah

Bay and the Santee, Waccamaw, Wando, Combahee, Edisto and Ashepoo Rivers. His first tidal-powered mill was built for Andrew Johnson on the North Santee in 1791; shortly thereafter the first steam-powered mill appeared. Other than the old rice field banks themselves, perhaps the most dramatic remnants of the rice industry today are the chimneys of rice mills, about a dozen of which remain in the Lowcountry. These tall, impressive brick structures served to draw heated air into a firebox and past a boiler to produce steam to power large horizontal steam engines. These stationary engines were mostly American-made, with several manufacturers located in Charleston.

Whether powered by wind, water, tidal flow or steam, mechanical mills required a significant capital investment and, as such, consolidation of rice processing occurred on the larger plantations and in urban areas, such as Georgetown and Charleston. With mechanization came obvious efficiency of production, but the cost of becoming a rice planter escalated. The rice kingdom consisted of no more than 100,000 planted acres at its peak in 1850. Rice planters numbered only about 550, and most of these were disproportionately wealthy. Most successful rice planters had "old money." By the early nineteenth century, prime rice land had become so expensive that the investment in land and slaves needed to begin a successful plantation was almost prohibitive. The shift to tidal production was principally an innovation of the elite, as only those already in the planter class could afford this costly expansion. The concentration of land in the hands of a few was also matched by a concentration of human property.

There is little doubt that the rice industry, with its dependence on a large, regimented, low-cost labor force, could not have flourished without the institution of slavery. Some, or perhaps most, of the slaves were from the west or windward coast of Africa, where they were familiar with rice cultivation. Slaves from West Africa along the Niger River in the interior and the coastal tropical rain forest were preferred in the slave markets by rice growers because they possessed knowledge of rice production. Undoubtedly, many of their skills were highly useful. Of all the crops planted in the colonial and antebellum period, rice was by far the most labor intensive. Some of the most prosperous planters owned upward of one thousand bondsmen. Demands of this labor-intensive industry were so voracious that, whereas in 1680, just prior to the introduction of rice, 83.4 percent of the South Carolina population was white, by 1708 the white population became the minority and remained so throughout the rice era.

Work was allotted each laborer taking into account skills and physical condition. An able-bodied slave would work as a "full hand." Those with less capability worked as "half hands" or "quarter hands." Rice fields were divided by small ditches into units known as "squares." Routinely, a full hand was responsible for a *single square, which was ordinarily about one acre in size. Work was assigned by the task labor system, a system probably originating in Africa, as it was a feature of African slavery along the windward coast as well as in the Caribbean islands during the Atlantic slave-trade era. The task system evolved as the principal method of labor management and organization on rice plantations. Once the allotted work was completed, the laborer had no other job responsibilities for the remainder of the day. This allowed for inter-plantation economy such as small-scale gardening, animal husbandry and fishing, managed by the slaves themselves for their own subsistence and profit.*

As a rice plantation was a particularly complex and self-sufficient enterprise, the specialized, skilled workforce included carpenters, blacksmiths, coopers and mechanics, as well as domestic staff. The highest rank among the slaves was that of foreman or "driver," requiring work in close concert with the white plantation manager. The driver was a privileged and trusted slave whose job was to assign tasks and make sure that they were completed to satisfaction. His job required a delicate balance—excessive discipline led to labor force demoralization, and excessive leniency and familiarity resulted in reduced productivity. The next in importance in the organization of the labor force was the "trunk minder." This individual was responsible for managing and monitoring the water levels in the fields.

Finally, in Georgetown, Charleston, Beaufort and Savannah, agents known as "factors" completed the economic structure. These businessmen acted as facilitators for the planters in the interface between their crop and the ultimate market. The factor's most important job was the successful sale of the crop. Since the rice planter himself was often not able, because of experience, temperament or location, to carry out the numerous activities associated with what was, in fact, a fairly complex business operation, these agents were indispensable.

The majority of the planters were of English origin, but over half of the original planters came by way of Barbados and neighboring islands where there was no room for further expansion. A small population of wealthy elite had emerged in that region of small islands during the 1640s, when sugar cane was introduced from Brazil.

Barbados's socio-economic model of slavery-based wealth, which rapidly accrued to a few individuals, was in large fashion replicated in Carolina a half century later. In addition, due to Carolina's relatively tolerant religious policy, Huguenots who could worship as they wished were attracted to the colony and many subsequently become planters.

By their very nature, rice plantations were established in hostile environments. Although some of the West African slaves were partially tolerant of malaria, yellow fever and a host of other diseases abetted by the poorly drained, unsanitary environment resulted in horrific amounts of illness and mortality. In addition,

periodic flooding often resulted in frequent drownings. For the most part, populations of slave communities were not self-sustaining; infant and adult mortalities required a steady influx of new individuals to maintain a constant workforce.

Sharing many of the same health hazards, if not the physical challenges, white overseers experienced a very high mortality rate, as well. On average, these young white males lasted only a few years before they and their families were either overtaken by illness or death or moved on to a more attractive position. There is little evidence that overseers frequently moved up to the ranks of plantation owners. Though the law required that one white overseer be employed per plantation unit, in many instances this was ignored, as often planters had more trust in their black slave drivers than in their white overseers.

The owners normally only visited their properties from November, at the end of the harvest, to early April, at the beginning of the planting stage. Plantations were justifiably feared as lethal during the summer months, as they were breeding grounds for the anopheles mosquito, the unrecognized vector for malaria. Summer homes for planters were often located in the healthier, upland piney woods, or along seashores. Many lived at beach communities, such as Edisto Island and Pawleys Island. Among the inland communities were the aptly named Plantersville and Summerville. For the more affluent, there were summer colonies to the north in such states as North Carolina, New York and Rhode Island.

Rice growing could be enormously profitable. On the eve of the American Revolution, the white population of the Lowcountry was by far the richest single group in colonial America, and, by extension, on average probably the wealthiest in the world. Nowhere else in America did a segment of the population live so well. Not only were they privileged to enjoy handsome residences in Charleston and elsewhere, but they were often able to travel and vacation in the North or abroad. Education of young men in Europe was

commonplace. Luxury goods of all sorts were readily available.

However, in spite of the spectacular local economic success of the rice planters, the rice industry itself was never of great importance to the colonies as a whole. It trailed sugar, cotton and tobacco by a large margin.

At the time of the War between the States, the Lowcountry economy was so structured that alternative economic activities could hardly be envisioned. This was an industry dependent on bound labor that produced a good for extra-regional consumption in a land of swamps and bogs that had very little alternative usage. Although economies of scale had been developed and mechanization introduced, quite simply it became cheaper to produce rice in Louisiana, Arkansas and Texas. In these *states, the land was firmer and thus better able to support farm machinery; double crops were often possible, allowing for larger yields. East India and lower Burma swamped the European rice markets by the late 1800s, in spite of the fact that the American product excelled in quality. Emancipation, of course, resulted in a breakdown of labor discipline and availability. This, combined with a long-term decline in soil fertility and a series of disastrous hurricanes, especially the one of 1893, ultimately led to the collapse of the rice industry and the whole Lowcountry economy. Just as rice had made the Lowcountry wealthy, it was rice that caused its demise. There was nothing to take its place.*

South Carolina planters and merchants did not give up on rice without a struggle, in spite of the devastation that followed the War between the States. However, the lack of capital and a specialized infrastructure made the development of an alternative industry just about impossible. The rice industry was nearly gone by the 1900s. The last commercial crop of rice was planted on the Combahee River by Theodore Ravenel in 1927.

In 1951 a group of Texas rice growers reintroduced commercial rice growing to South Carolina, particularly along the Combahee and Edisto Rivers. "New Prospects of Rice Crop Have Low Country in a Tizzy," proclaimed the September 10, 1951 Savannah Morning News. *Optimism also*

abounded in the Beaufort and Charleston papers. But in spite of a great deal of local support and enthusiasm, these enterprises did not succeed.

After the rice plantations fell into disuse, in most instances their banks were broached and the water-control structures became inoperable. Many of these plantations passed into the hands of wealthy Northern sportsmen who sometimes restored and rebuilt the rice fields, primarily for waterfowl shooting. They sometimes also planted rice on a small scale to perpetuate its glories.

With the demise of the rice industry in the Lowcountry, Carolina Gold seemed to disappear. But this was not to be the case. Some seed was apparently carried to South America by Confederate war veterans. Quite remarkably,

"Carolina Doro" has recently been discovered being grown by slash-and-burn farmers in the Amazon basin. Likewise, it appears that Carolina Gold was introduced to West Africa during a period of black repatriations, as there exists a variety known as "Mereki," a distortion of the name America. Research has shown this grain to have similar gene structure to Carolina Gold. Other small amounts of seed were packaged and kept as heirlooms by descendants of planters. Finally, some seed samples found their way into gene banks in agricultural research stations.

That's where I found Carolina Gold in 1985.

Part II

The Rebirth of Rice in the Lowcountry

*S*ome years ago, I purchased a small plantation on the Wright River in Jasper County, South Carolina. The area once known as Tunbridge is located on the upper regions of the river, where it comprises approximately four hundred acres of tidal marsh, freshwater impoundments, open fields and woods. Abundant Native American artifacts bear evidence to its innate productivity. Plentiful wildlife indicates that even now, in spite of the encroachments of civilization, it is a very bountiful environment. Though only four air miles from the city of

Savannah, there are places that appear to be total wilderness.

I bought the property in the early 1970s, renamed it Turnbridge, as the landing at the corner of the property had come to be known, and established a retreat from the city life of Savannah, where I practice as an Ophthalmologist. What made the place especially appealing to me was the presence of impoundments, formed over old rice fields, which could be managed for duck hunting. With the demise of the rice industry, the property had fallen into disuse, although at one time the back entrance road had been re-engineered to accommodate a previous owner's limousine, as smuggling Scotch whisky through Turnbridge Landing in the 1930s had brought a brief revival of prosperity. Subsequent owners had rebuilt and maintained the rice fields, fortunately, as the reclamation of rice field banks has now been prohibited for a number of years. The headwaters of the Wright River have been blocked by the Army Corps of Engineers, who dredged the Savannah River; this resulted in the narrowing of the river at this point and a drastic increase in salinity. Thus, the tidal-flow system of water management, which had once been in place, was rendered impossible, as rice is not salt tolerant.

I appreciated none of the aforementioned, and naively assumed that flooded fields meant a myriad of ducks.

Predictably, my first few seasons of duck hunting were not very productive, but they were immensely pleasurable. I began to pour more and more effort into enhancing the habitat.

Along the way I became convinced that rice growing in the fields would be the magic ingredient to attract ducks, just as historical accounts of the sport suggested. On the strength of this hypothesis, I decided to grow rice.

Working at Turnbridge was a friend and neighbor, Julius Bing. Julius's credentials as a rice grower were not overly impressive. A retired truck driver for the U.S. Government Printing Office in Washington, D.C., and the son of a former employee of a regional railroad, Julius must have counted among his distant ancestors slaves who had worked in rice fields, but certainly none of their prior knowledge or experience could have been

genetically imparted. My credentials were even less impressive. My ancestors were ranchers in Texas and tobacco growers in Virginia, but my father had left the family ranch at an early age to become a research scientist. His agricultural interest extended only to prize camellias. In spite of an undergraduate degree in biology, I knew nothing whatsoever about farming, let alone something as complex as rice growing. About the only useful things that Julius and I brought to the project were a great deal of energy, enthusiasm and patience. But they are of huge importance.

The other ingredient needed to grow rice was, of course, a proper field. This we did have and fortunately they were in fairly good condition, since the banks had been rebuilt and maintained by the previous owners. The original rice field impoundments were a structural nightmare, as they were usually quite flimsy, being constructed by hand out of soil with a high organic content. The earlier rice field banks were kept devoid of trees, as these might topple over in a high wind and thus rip out a plug in the wall, resulting in an instant leak, which could quickly erode. In addition, the peaty soil could easily wash away with storm-driven high tides or even burn. Our modern banks were machine-made, wide enough to accommodate vehicular traffic, and able to support trees, making them aesthetically more appealing.

Our water-control structures were much simpler than the originals because they didn't have to do the same work. Thanks to the altered salinity in the Wright River, water from the river could no longer be used to flood crops. In fact, the brackish water, which was about one-fourth the strength seawater, was quite useful to flood some of the other ponds, which enabled widgeon grass, an excellent duck food, to flourish. The only sources of fresh water were thus rain and a large, deep well. Our water-control devices consisted of metal trunks called "flashboard risers" with which the water height could be adjusted by placing planks in a slot attached to a pipe that ran under the rice field bank. The use of a well for flooding was more reliable than earlier trunks, but, on the other hand, it worked a good bit slower. We had the fields and the enthusiasm, now we needed the seed and a little bit of guidance.

The seed was the easiest part. A phone call to Gifford's Feed & Seed in Estill, South Carolina, procured a few bags of Labelle seed, *a genetically engineered, modern variety of low-height, disease-resistant, high-yield rice.*

Guidance was more of a challenge. Dan and Kenny Bryan at the top of the road had a lifetime of experience growing things in the Lowcountry, as did Keith White, the manager at neighboring Delta Plantation. None of them, however, had ever grown rice. Joe Harrison Sr., a retired banker at nearby Fife Plantation, had actually grown rice on a small scale for many years and was an invaluable source of help. Tommy Walker of the Clemson University Cooperative Extension Service was able to obtain rice production booklets, as well as provide information on a number of details, such as planting dates, fertilization amounts and herbicide schedules. Historical accounts of

Lowcountry rice growing were, for the most part, not particularly helpful, as we certainly were not about to try to replicate many of the early agricultural practices. In large part, grueling human and animal energy would have to be replaced by internal combustion engines and modern farm equipment.

Having gathered as much information as possible, we were able to grow rice on one six-acre field. It was not a very productive crop and was a bit weedy, but it was nonetheless a field of rice. And then, at the end of the growing season, we flooded it again and waited for the clouds of ducks to descend. They didn't come. They couldn't have cared less. At that time, I

was unaware of the role that ducks had once played in the cycle of early rice growing.

Ducks were attracted to the early fields in great numbers, but were prized not for sport or the table, but for an entirely different reason. Traditionally, the trunk minder, a trusted and reliable monitor of water levels, was supplied with a musket and charged with shooting a few ducks for the master's table. The rest were encouraged to stay and feed on the residual grain, which was inevitably left behind with the harvest. One of the major weed problems of early rice growers was red rice. Red rice plants vary considerably and most produce a dark seed. When milled rice is contaminated with these dark grains, the market value is diminished. Botanically, red rice is the same species as cultivated rice, but this rogue variety is a fierce competitor, thereby reducing crop yield. Since it is the same species as the desirable rice and grows in the same manner, little could be done to prevent its growth once established. One difference between the two, however, is that most red rice shatters before harvest time and, thus, almost all of the seed remains in the field. Left alone, there will be a heavy infestation the following year and further reduction in crop yield. Here, certain types of waterfowl, known as puddle or dabbling ducks, came to the rescue. If the rice fields were flooded to a depth of a foot or two, birds, such as mallards, pintails, widgeon and teal, would consume much of the residual seed by tipping in the shallow water. Since much of the remaining seed was that of red rice, its emergence the following season could be drastically reduced by allowing the birds to feed on the seeds. To the best of my knowledge, we have not been plagued with red rice, as all of our sources of seed have been free of the contaminant.

In spite of what seemed to be a hopeless waste of time by a couple of total amateurs, there were some aspects of rice growing that somehow captured my imagination and Julius's. It was hard on people and tough on the farm equipment, but it was, in its own way, rewarding to see rice growing where it once had flourished. Maybe the ducks would change their minds and maybe I wouldn't give up just yet.

And then I read a couple of interesting things. The first was a wonderfully comprehensive article in, of all things, the New Yorker magazine. Written by E.J. Kahn Jr., this *treatise on rice mentioned that scientists were actively studying the genetics of rice and that some sixty-five thousand varieties of rice had been accessioned and stored for future studies in several institutions. About the same time, I read the label that accompanied my modern hybrid rice and discovered that Carolina Gold was in its pedigree. It didn't take much imagination to thus assume that somewhere, someone must have some of the original seed from Madagascar.*

On the strength of this assumption, I contacted the Rice Council in Houston, Texas, and they directed me to Dr. Charles N. Bollich, a rice research scientist with the United States Department of Agriculture in Beaumont, Texas. Dr. Bollich did, indeed, have in his collection Carolina Gold and he very generously grew some for me. In 1985, I received two small bags of seed rice totalling fourteen pounds. It was exactly three hundred years after another surgeon in South Carolina was given a peck of seed. As a peck is one-quarter of a bushel, and rice not hulled averages about forty-five pounds to the bushel, Dr. Woodward likely started with about eleven pounds. Quite a coincidence, but given my inexperience, I needed that three-pound advantage.

In 1985, I planted none of my hybrid rice in preparation for the reintroduction of Carolina Gold. Even though rice naturally self-fertilizes, different varieties can cross readily, so isolation is required. In the spring of 1986,

I planted the entire contents of Dr. Bollich's two bags in a small pond. This impoundment, which had once held a catfish operation, had been carefully prepared with attention to grade and drainage. The soil was fertilized, limed and then planted with a seeder known as a grain drill in mid-April. In no time at all, lines of little green stalks appeared. Shortly thereafter, additional fertilizer in the form of dry urea was broadcast over the little field and then well water was added. As the plants grew and matured, I raised the water level to act as a natural weed control and also to support the long stems.

Once the plants were fully matured in early September, the water was drained away slowly, leaving a crop that roughly resembled wheat. We were then presented with the challenge of harvesting the rice. Rather than resorting to the original methods of cutting bundles of rice manually with rice hooks, we hit upon the idea of simply stripping the seeds directly from the stalk by hand. We quickly discovered that whole-grain rice is extremely abrasive. When we tried to strip it with our bare hands, our skin quickly began to wear away. Thus we resorted to wearing heavy leather gloves and transferring the grains to carpenters' nail aprons. This was quite uncomfortable work made more difficult by heat and insects. Although our first production did not multiply by biblical proportions, we were able to achieve a substantial increase in seed. In spite of the obvious temptation, none of the sixty-four pounds of harvested Carolina Gold made its way to the table.

The following year we repeated the process, but now in two catfish ponds. Again the yield was substantial, so this time we were able to enlist a local farmer, Richard Crosby, to combine the rice. We had worked our way up to 470 pounds.

By 1988, we were well on our way. The catfish pond nurseries were abandoned and we planted a full rice field with a yield of about five thousand pounds. With the harvest of this crop, we were now in a position to process it for the table. Rice grain in its natural form is known as "paddy" or "rough rice." Surrounding the starchy endosperm, which is the edible part, are layers of bran and a tough hull. Once removed from the field, it is necessary to clean and dry the grain and then remove the hull and polish off the bran. Of course, all of the commercial rice mills in South Carolina had long since vanished. There were real logistical challenges to getting a small amount of paddy to the closest mills in Arkansas. Fortunately, Remer Lane Sr., the father of a good friend, had an old rice huller left over from his days as owner of Combahee Plantation. Through his generosity, we were able to mill the rice.

At long last the fabled grain could be tasted. Tricia, my wife and co-worker, arranged a reintroduction banquet at the Oglethorpe Club in Savannah in December 1988. Four dozen friends joined to discover that the rice did, indeed, live up to its reputation. A variety of rice dishes, all the way through to rice pudding dessert, confirmed, without a doubt, that Carolina Gold was indeed something very special.

A week or so later in the Living section of the New York Times, *John Martin Taylor, a food historian and writer from Charleston, published a feature article entitled "Carolina Gold: A rare harvest," establishing the notoriety of our project. Not wishing this to be a commercial venture, Tricia and I donated the rice to the Savannah Association for the Blind. A life-altering project filled with frustrations, disappointments and physical hardships, but also immense gratification, was launched.*

Often, during wet weather, one of my patients will inquire about my rice project and ask if I can get into my rice fields. My answer is

always the same, "Of course I can, but I won't be able to get back out." One of the causes for the collapse of the rice industry in South Carolina was that the fields were unsuitable for early mechanized farm machinery. Many Lowcountry rice fields will not support heavy farm machinery of any sort. Our fields, on the other hand, are somewhat amenable to tractor traffic, as they have a clay substrata beneath the topsoil that gives relatively good support. Nevertheless, rain is quite often a source of frustration and the fields never seem to dry fast enough. At every stage in our rice production, rain is the single biggest problem.

At the end of the winter months, a skim of water, which has been kept on the fallow rice fields to attract snipe, is drained away through water-control structures known as flashboard risers. A practical and inexpensive means of doing this is to attach a tractor tire inner tube to the river side of the riser drainage pipe. Rising tidewater simply collapses the inner tube and when the tide ebbs the field water percolates through.

Once drained and dried, the fields are ready to be burned—not a particularly easy project. On the insides of the banks are "face ditches," which drain into the flashboard risers. They are just a little too wide to jump over and ordinarily hold some water. They are thus a reasonable firebreak unless there is a significant wind shift and the fire becomes explosive. The banks on the other side are not combustible, but the trees on them are vulnerable, especially cedars, so great care must be exercised in containing the fire.

Controlled burning, which must be done with a permit from the fire service, is a hazardous business. Should a fire escape the confines of our rice fields, there are no close natural barriers of containment. Since much of the surrounding area is marshland, which can, under the right circumstances, be highly combustible, each burning operation is approached with some apprehension. Yet in spite of the risks, burning is worthwhile because it reduces the heavy mat of rice stalks, puts nutrients back into the soil and reduces the insect population.

After drying and burning, the fields are then ready for preparation of the seedbed. Originally this was done in small plots by hoe and without applying fertilizer. In our case, we incorporate fertilizer into the soil, utilizing a tractor pulling a disc harrow. It is ordinarily necessary to cut the soil several times to create a smooth surface of bare dirt. Weather permitting, planting takes place in mid-April. This was the traditional rice planting time in South Carolina, although there was considerable variation among individual planters. The principal reason for the April date was that this enabled the plants to establish prior to the annual migration of "ricebirds." Those members of the blackbird family, known as bobolinks, have now all but disappeared from the Carolina coast and have moved their range inland. It was quite an event a number of years ago when we spotted a small flock of them.

The actual planting of the rice is done on dry soil using a grain drill. This consists of a tractor-pulled container, which feeds seed into devices that deliver a steady stream of grain into shallow openings in the soil created by small spinning disks. A trailing chain and rings gently cover the seed. The grain drill is adjustable for the rate of delivery. We have found that a rate of ninety-six pounds to the acre, or about two bushels, gives the best results. This method of planting is similar to what is now done in the real world of modern commercial rice farming in this country.

Once the field is planted, there is little to do but wait for rain. This can be an agonizing period. If the rain does not come and the plants begin to germinate without adequate moisture, at least partial crop failure is certain. As we have to rely on our well and it is not of a capacity to allow a quick flush of water, this is a particularly vulnerable time for the crop.

Some three weeks after emergence, the rice grows to about six inches. We top dress with additional fertilizer in the form of dry urea delivered by a spin spreader. At the same time, herbicides are sprayed to control competing grasses and broad-leaf weeds. In the past, weed control was carried out by a combination of intermittent flooding and hand hoeing; in our case, modern chemicals rescue us from an unbelievably arduous task. At this point, the well is cut on and the flashboard risers are closed and sealed.

The process of flooding begins.

Rice can be grown on dry land without controlled flood, but it is not very productive

when done this way. So-called "providence rice"
was commonly grown for home consumption in
the wet part of other crop fields throughout the
coastal Southeast. We have one such low area
in an upland field on Turnbridge that has been
planted with modern rice seed in recent memory.
Many of my older patients recall their families
planting providence rice, with only sporadic
success. The topography of upland crop fields
in the Lowcountry is rarely level, but given the
right circumstances it may be possible in a
dry spring for rice to be planted in a low boggy
area and then have enough subsequent rain to
produce a crop, but this is mostly a matter of
chance. Productivity is low.

As flooding takes place, the rice stalks rise
ahead of the water level. If heavy rains occur and
cover the rice, it is necessary to drop the level, as

rice can, in fact, be drowned. Carolina Gold is a tall plant so it is necessary to flood to a knee-deep level to cover most of the stalk. Shortly after flooding is completed, the plants begin to head out, with the emergence of immature green-colored seed. As the grain develops, the contents are liquid in form, known as the "milk stage." This is a quite accurate description, for when the grain is squeezed between the fingers, a milky substance is expressed. It is this rice milk that was so attractive to the now-departed bobolinks. Their place, however, has been filled by hordes of red-winged blackbirds. These birds are quite remarkable in their ability to hover almost like hummingbirds, clutching the rice stalk, which will not support their weight, while they suck the milk out of the young rice seeds. Clouds of these pests descend together on the fields in spite of all of our attempts to frighten them away. We finally accepted the reality that they are going to take a certain percentage of the crop. I suspect the actual percentage of loss is quite considerable, but since there is nothing that we can effectively do about it, we really don't want to know.

Although it is a pointless exercise, ricebirds are quite easily shot. One simply aims a shotgun at the flock, pulls the trigger, and down come a dozen or so birds. At one time they were harvested as a collateral crop and considered a great delicacy, being brought to market in strings of a dozen and sold for pennies. Some planters expended great effort to frighten the pests away using slaves as "bird minders" to create incessant noise, *but I suspect that most, like us, just altered their planting dates to minimize the loss.*

As maturation proceeds and the grain hardens, a most remarkable visual transformation occurs. The stems and leaves, which are lime green, contrast sharply with the grain heads, which turn to a golden brown. Best appreciated in low ambient light in the early morning or late evening, the fields become a sea of shimmering, glittering gold. A gentle breeze can add to the effect. Hence the name is derived from the plant's appearance and not the economic impact that the crop once had on the Lowcountry.

One of our greatest joys has been the visual treat afforded by the golden rice. We have been visited by many talented photographers who have achieved some remarkable work. They, like numerous visiting writers, have been entertaining in their own right. Perhaps most memorable was a photographic team from the BBC, who visited us having just photographed Aboriginal rock paintings in Australia. They were next slated to do endoscopic photography of the restoration of the Portland vase at the British Museum.

Carolina Gold is a very long-stemmed plant, as opposed to shorter modern varieties. This characteristic creates the problem of "lodging," or the collapsing of the plants in a house-of-cards fashion. While undergoing *maturation and gaining weight at the top of the plant, the surrounding water provides support. Strong winds can, however, blow the crop down and it can, as well, be toppled by wildlife, especially deer. If the grain heads end up on the floor of the field, they deteriorate and are lost.*

Once fully matured, the leaves and stems begin to turn from green to tan and the crop loses much of its visual luster. At this point, the water is very slowly drained off the fields. If this is done too quickly, more lodging may occur. Birds continue their deprecation and, as a result, some of the grains fall to the ground, where they become an attraction to short-nosed cotton rats and, by extension, water moccasins. Walking through the fields at this stage with poor visibility below can be an intimidating experience. On more than one occasion, Julius and I have had unpleasant encounters with these snakes. Although Turnbridge is home to a very robust population of alligators, including some huge individuals, they never posed any problems that we recognized, and probably kept the snakes somewhat in check.

Surprisingly, modern rice fields are not breeding grounds for mosquitoes, as plowing and disking of the fields interferes with their breeding cycle. This does not mean, however, that we are not plagued with them, as we have ample salt marshes and wetlands surrounding the fields, which produce not only mosquitoes, but the more troublesome deer flies. In the past, however, hand-cultivated rice fields whose soil was not uniformly disturbed were

recognized as breeding grounds for disease. In 1817, for instance, the Georgia Medical Society successfully sponsored the prohibition of wet rice cultured within a radius of one mile of the city limits of Savannah. The result was a reported dramatic improvement in public health.

Harvesting has been the single most difficult and frustrating aspect of our rice operation. Our rice fields have a substrata of buckshot clay, which when reasonably dry will support heavy machinery. Once dry, the fields won't stay that way, as periodic fall rains are a near certainty. Tricia and I early on made the strategic decision not to own a combine. These are expensive, high-maintenance machines, which are quite dangerous with their myriad of moving parts. They are only used for a day or so each year. To solidify that decision, we even constructed a new equipment shed with dimensions that would not accommodate a combine. We were thus left at the mercy of the few people in our area who still farm and are willing to rent their machines and staff. Some were reliable, but others were not. Combines are cumbersome machines that move slowly on the highway; transplanting them to Turnbridge was awkward and inefficient. Dry fields and ideal harvesting conditions were often wasted due to broken promises and delays until the rains came; when water re-accumulated the crop yield deteriorated. Once in the field, the machines invariably broke down as storm clouds gathered. We have never had a harvest that went off without a hitch and some have been such disasters that we were barely able to recover enough seed to plant the following year.

Historically, rice yields of about one thousand pounds to the acre were the norm. Our production in good years has hardly ever exceeded that. Since rice heads contain more than one hundred grains, and we plant about one hundred pounds per acre, our theoretic potential yield would be something on the order of ten thousand pounds to the acre. In modern rice areas using hybrid varieties, this level of production is approached. This is a good indication of our lack of efficiency and the limited yield potential of Carolina Gold. At the very worst, when we have had a year of crop failure and a poor yield, we strive to gather at least twelve hundred pounds of usable rice to serve as seed for the following year's planting in twelve acres.

The combines we have used were designed for small-grain harvest, such as wheat. They are not modified for wet-field operation and thus can easily bog down. Spinning paddles on the front gather in the grain, along with bits of leaves, stems, weeds, grasshoppers and the like. This has a high moisture content and requires immediate cleaning and drying. Fortunately, the Harper Bower Mill in Estill had an adequate facility, left over from the short period of rice revival on the Combahee River in the 1950s. When this mill closed a few years ago, we had to resort to other facilities, often with some very disastrous results. On one occasion, a good harvest was delivered to another mill and then was totally ruined when the grain was left in an open truck

during a three-day rain. A year's effort was lost through simple carelessness.

Once dried, the rice is bagged in fifty-pound sacks while twelve hundred pounds are set aside, treated with fungicides and stored for next year's seed. We then deal with the remaining dried rice for one of the most pleasant aspects of the project. Rough rice in the hull is not edible and must be milled. Rough rice or paddy grain contains an outer protective layer known as the husk, which accounts for 20 to 22 percent of the grain weight. After the husk is removed, the internal kernel, known as brown or de-husked rice, contains an additional fibrous covering called bran, which constitutes another 8 to 10 percent of the weight. Just as the hard woody husk is inedible and must be removed, the bran, which is also difficult to cook and digest, is also removed by additional milling called "polishing" or "whitening." Rice milling is thus the process of removing the husk and the bran in order to produce an edible product.

Considering the relatively small amount of product to be processed, the only practical way to complete our project was to mill on site. Fortunately, Keith White, the manager at neighboring Delta Plantation, knew of an old mill in nearby Ridgeland, South Carolina. The machine had not been used for many years and sat in the back of a derelict warehouse with a collapsing floor. The widow of the previous owner was contacted and a *sale was affected. Keith and my son Richard Jr. were able to extricate the mill with a great deal of difficulty by laying down boards on the floor beams and sliding it out to our truck. It was then delivered to the shop at Turnbridge for restoration. Made in Syracuse, New York, in the late 1800s, the Engelberg rice huller was the product of a now-extinct company. Remarkably, most of the machine was intact and even more remarkable, the operating instructions printed on a paper label attached to the machine were still legible. As this machine has its own peculiarities, having a full set of instructions proved most valuable. Equally valuable was the gift of the few missing parts through the generosity of the Harrison family. Years ago, a barn at their Fife Plantation containing an identical mill had burned down. The remains of the destroyed mill lay in a pile under a nearby oak tree. We were able to scrounge through the rubble and come up with the needed parts.*

Restoration took place in our shop alongside a 1932 automobile that was being rebuilt. No effort was made to do anything cosmetic to the machine. All efforts were directed to a full mechanical restoration to put it in first-class working order. Originally, power was delivered through a belt drive from a steam or internal combustion engine. The instructions included the optimal rpm and we were able to fit a five-horsepower electric engine with the appropriate-size drive wheel to produce the desired speed. An undercarriage with casters for mobility was fitted and we were in the rice-milling business.

The machine basically consists of two parts—a hulling cylinder and a polishing drum. Rice is placed into a hopper on top of the hulling cylinder and then fed into a rotating chamber where the abrasive rice hulls are agitated against one another to knock the hulls off the grain. The hull fragments are separated through a screen and expelled while the grains then drop down into the polishing drum. There, little leather fingers beat against the grains to remove the bran. The finished product is then discharged into a container as white rice.

Rice hulling has turned out to be a most relaxing and pleasant activity. The old machine is capable of producing two hundred pounds of finished rice an hour, during which time it produces a most soothing, rhythmic sound and an appealing aroma, not unlike that of freshly baked bread. It has a number of adjustments and all of us—Tricia, Julius, Richard Jr. and I—have our own ideas about how to run and adjust it. Usually the mill works best on cold, dry evenings. Some days more rice is broken than others, but in general a large percentage of the grains are shattered.

Carolina Gold did not enjoy a good reputation with millers, as it had a strong propensity for breakage. Broken rice, although undistinguishable to the palate, commanded only a fraction of the price of whole grain rice. Collected in five-gallon buckets at the bottom of the mill, the rice is stored in large, closed plastic containers. In spite of vigorous attempts to control weeds in the fields and aggressive cleaning of the combine, an amazingly large number of weed seeds end up in the final product. As these *seeds are dark in color, they can easily be spotted and removed when the rice is in the kitchen.*

Early on we contacted the United States Department of Agriculture and asked them to inspect our operation. Needless to say, they were aghast when they found us milling rice in the same shop where we were restoring an old car. These deficiencies could, of course, be rectified, but there remained another problem. In 1956, the South Carolina legislature passed a law requiring all rice sold within the state to have added vitamins and minerals. Delicious as it may be, rice lacks many important nutrients, especially if it is highly milled. Since rice is a traditional staple food for many people in the coastal South, enriching the product can provide nutritional improvements for the population. These additives are water soluble, so to add them to our rice, which should be washed several times in preparation, would be futile. This re-enforced our decision not to make this a commercial project, and our rice is instead given to friends and patients in small quantities and given to charities to sell at a price considerably higher than ordinary rice. None of our product would grace the tables of the nutritionally deprived in any significant amount. Fortunately this regulation, which was appropriate in its time, has recently been rescinded.

The final step in our production is to bag the rice. Attractive one-pound sacks with drawstrings are filled by volunteers at the designated charities. Supplies *permitting, the rice is also distributed to our patients, many of whom appear to be more enamored with the container than the product. In the meantime, the rice fields are not neglected.*

In the fall, after the harvest and with no further manipulation, we re-flood the fields to attract ducks.

Richard Jr., who has now taken possession of Turnbridge, mows the rice stubble prior to re-flooding, with much better duck-shooting success than Tricia and I have had. Julius Bing is now sadly departed, as is Joe Harrison. Keith White has moved away. Leroy Bentley is now helping

Richard Jr., who has taken a big step forward with the acquisition of a combine.

Good year and bad year, the challenges and joys associated with rice persist. Its beauty is stunning. Its taste is divine and in greater or lesser numbers, the ducks continue their annual visits.

Bibliography

Bagwell, James E. *Rice Gold: James Hamilton Couper and Plantation Life on the Georgia Coast.* Macon, Georgia: Mercer University Press, 2000.

Burney, Eugenia. *Colonial South Carolina.* Nashville, Tennessee: Thomas Nelson, 1970.

Carney, Judith A. *Black Rice: The African Origins of Rice Cultivation in the Americas.* Cambridge: Harvard University Press, 2001.

Coclanis, Peter A. *The Shadow of a Dream: Economic Life and Death in the South Carolina Low Country, 1670–1920.* New York: Oxford University Press, 1989.

Dethloff, Henry C. *A History of the American Rice Industry, 1685–1985.* College Station: Texas A&M University Press, 1988.

Doar, David. *Rice and Rice Planting in the South Carolina Low Country.* Charleston: The Charleston Museum, 1936.

Dawsey, Cyrus B., and James M. Dawsey. *The Confederados: Old South Immigrants in Brazil.* Tuscaloosa: University of Alabama Press, 1995.

Dusinberre, William. *Them Dark Days: Slavery in the American Rice Swamps.* New York: Oxford University Press, 1996.

Easterby, J.H., ed. *The South Carolina Rice Plantation as Revealed in the Papers of Robert F.W. Allston.* Chicago: University of Chicago Press, 1945.

Edgar, Walter. *South Carolina: A History.* Columbia: University of South Carolina Press, 1998.

Fitch, James A. *Pass the Pilau, Please.* Georgetown, South Carolina: The Rice Museum, 2001.

Granger, Mary, ed. *Savannah River Plantations: Savannah Writers' Project, 1947.* Spartanburg, South Carolina: The Reprint Company, 1983.

Hess, Karen. *The Carolina Rice Kitchen: The African Connection.* Columbia: University of South Carolina Press, 1992.

Heyward, Duncan Clinch. *Seed From Madagascar.* Chapel Hill: The University of North Carolina Press, 1937.

Hill, Max L. II. "Carolina Gold Rice Planting in the Low Country." Lecture, Men's Study Group, Charleston, South Carolina, October 1987.

Kahn, E.J. Jr. "The Staffs of Life IV: Everybody's Business," *New Yorker*, March 4, 1985.

Lawson, Dennis T. *No Heir to Take its Place: The Story of Rice in Georgetown County, South Carolina.* Georgetown, South Carolina: The Rice Museum, 1972.

Lee, F.D. and J.L. Agnew. *Historic Record of the City of Savannah*. Savannah: Morning News Steam Powered Press, 1869.

Littlefield, Daniel C. *Rice and Slaves: Ethnicity and the Slave Trade in Colonial South Carolina*. Urbana: University of Illinois Press, 1981.

————. "Rice and the Making of South Carolina: An Introductory Essay." Columbia: South Carolina. Department of Archives and History, 1995.

Marscher, Bill, and Fran Marscher. *The Great Sea Island Storm of 1893*. San Jose, California: Authors Choice Press, 2001.

Pennington, Patience. *A Woman Rice Planter*. New York: The Macmillan Co., 1914.

Porcher, Richard Dwight. "Rice Culture in South Carolina: A Brief History, the Role of the Huguenots, and Preservation of Its Legacy." Transactions of the Huguenot Society of South Carolina 92 (1987).

Potter, Eloise F. *Birds of the Carolinas*. Chapel Hill: The University of North Carolina Press, 1980.

Richards, T. Addison. "The Rice Lands of the South." *Harper's New Monthly Magazine* 114, November 1859.

Rowland, Lawrence S. "'Alone on the River': The Rise and Fall of the Savannah River Rice Plantations of St. Peter's Parish." *South Carolina Historical Magazine* 88 (July 1987): 121–50.

Rowland, Lawrence S., Alexander Moore, George C. Rogers, and George C. Rogers Jr. *The History of Beaufort County, South Carolina, Volume I: 1541–1861*. Columbia: University of South Carolina Press, 1996.

Salley, A.S. Jr. "The Introduction of Rice Culture into South Carolina." *Bulletins of the Historic Commission of South Carolina*, no. 6. Columbia: Printed for the Commission by the State Company, Columbia, South Carolina, 1919.

Smith, Julia Floyd. *Slavery and Rice Culture in Low Country Georgia, 1750–1860*. Knoxville: University of Tennessee Press, 1985.

Taylor, John Martin. "Carolina Gold: Rare Harvest." *The New York Times*, December 28, 1988.

Waldron, Ann. "Golden Harvest." *Princeton Alumni Weekly*, April 18, 1990.

Wilder, Effie Leland. *Henry Woodward, Forgotten Man of American History: A Sketch of South Carolina's Intrepid Pioneer*. Columbia, South Carolina: Sandlapper Press, 1970.